Lifting the Stone

Lifting the Stone

Susan McCaslin

To Elizabeth,

best wishes

Susan McCaslin

Seraphim Editions

The publisher gratefully acknowledges the financial assistance of the Canada Council for the Arts and the Ontario Arts Council.

The Canada Council | Le Conseil des Arts
for the Arts | du Canada

ONTARIO ARTS COUNCIL
CONSEIL DES ARTS DE L'ONTARIO

Library and Archives Canada Cataloguing in Publication

McCaslin, Susan, 1947-

    Lifting the stone / Susan McCaslin.

Poems.

ISBN 978-0-9735487-8-5

    I. Title.

PS8575.C43L53 2007   C811'.54   C2007-905663-6

Editor: Allan Briesmaster
Cover Photo: Pamela Williams
Author Photo: Mark Haddock
Cover Design and Typography: Julie McNeill, McNeill Design Arts

Published in 2007 by
Seraphim Editions
238 Emerald St. N.
Hamilton, ON
Canada L8L 5K8

Printed and bound in Canada

Cleave a piece of wood,
I am there;
Lift up the stone
And you will find me there.

– The Gospel of Thomas

For Mark

Contents

Codex

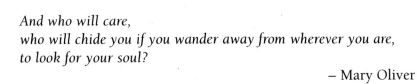

And who will care,
who will chide you if you wander away from wherever you are,
to look for your soul?

— Mary Oliver

If I/I Will

If I stand tiptoe and cup my hands around the moon
or reach deep into the shadows of my teens
and hear the turbulent morass
of my parents' warfare,

I withdraw again into a closet
or a world of tomes,
the fascinating rise and fall of print,
becoming again that nest of curled, inarticulate sounds –

refugee not even myself can fathom.

Brother

"You're not the student your sister was,"
one teacher remarked, so you clenched
your motor-oiled hands, not allowing
yourself words.

You are salt, water.
A voice inside ponders, "Who loves
me, cares for me?"
                              Adrift
in your old blue Ford
when Dad was wasting, you shouldered
his bones like an eighteenth-century ploughman.

"No surprises," you pleaded,
"don't let this one shake me" –
then cradled him as his soul flew out.

When you called with the report,
your voice was a hand on a solid brass
doorknob, looking for the next opening.

"He's gone," you said, but didn't add –
          "and you in Lotus land."

Shedding and Clinging

Like a garden snake rubbing its belly on fallen sheath,
one must shed and cling in a single motion.

My mother did it in '59
when she sold the heavy mahogany furniture,
flew west, found herself rotating in Seattle
in a Danish-modern chair.

(The hoarders and profligates in hell
wedded forever in hungry alliance.)

Better to let the manna pass lightly through –
Kiss it as it flies

Shun the Thorn, Cull the Fruit

The blackberry, that most pernicious vine,
crept over from the neighbour's side of the fence
enmeshing itself in my delicate Japanese maple.

I hacked and pulled against taut ropes of thorns
till one, suddenly slackening in my hands,
threw me like a wrestler on my back.

Arms raw with scratches kept on
attacking Jack's path to Giantland,
daring Sleeping Beauty's hedge,

but in time, the troubling vine burst back
huger than before, dropping blue-black
globes of sweetness to my hands.

Why should this thick beast
I could not exorcise the year before
now crown me with its superflux of fruit?

Summer Godlore

In this green necklace of a summer
where days are peridots,
I am my own blockage and release,

a dike unhinged into the godflow,
a stipple in Noon's Creek.
Vials of sleep may cure what words cannot.

Two birds – one thought, one feeling,
cling to the tree of the body.
Don't ask me to choose between them.

Three Vegetarians Tour a Venison Farm

Our distant relative, this Oxfordshire farmer,
didn't have the least idea we were vegetarians,
spurners of his hearty venison,

but here we are on the back of his four-wheeler
touring his fields of red deer who bounce gracefully
like the wild ones in British Columbia,
mule deer and blacktail in the forest near our home.

In fog-patched light spotted fawns nestle in grassbeds,
perched briefly on gangly legs. My daughter,
beside me on the truck, stretches
toward the flicker of velvet ears
and would make pets of them all.

The farmer mutters "harvest" and "slaughter,"
but she doesn't catch the words through his accent,
so the rest of us carry for her the knowledge
of their ten- to twelve-month lifespan in the fields,

and of the hour he herds them into a truck
and waves them off as his father did before him,
an honest man doing what he must,
having been raised to it.

Yet something in him is a frozen lake
closed to the gentleness of the deer –
their delicate regard.

How My Students Inspire Poetic Thinking

"Black Elk falls into a comma
and receives a vision," writes one,
and another expounds how Black Elk hears voices
"beaconing him,"

so I am dreamily beaconed by the light of tidal winds
that weep me into long-drawn commas,
pulled into the endlessness between letters
down ellipses of stars, stairs,
no longer poetically marginalized
by my own marginal commentary.

How the poet loves the hands that uttered these gifts,
enough to enter, if not a vision,
then, a kind of tranced stepping to the end of the essay
where she inscribes the niggling B- or C+

– faint recompense for such unconscious mining.

Cribbed from My Students' Essays

(a found poem)

Suddenly,
a squirmish arose on the streets of Verona.

Unfortunately
Shakespeare writes a series of unfortunate events
in which Othello falls for Iago's inseminations.

The more traditional Desdemona
on the other hand
makes tragic circumstances occur
when she is totally unaware
of any malicious depravations
on the part of Othello

even to the point where he is strangling her.

She helps tragic circumstances arise again
when her innocence and passive feminine traits are clashed
against Othello's aggressive boldness.

(Centuries ago, men were the prevenlent gender
and held the most power in society.)

Romeo
on another hand, takes immediate action
by climbing the balcony in order to have
a few intimidated moments with Juliet.

He puts her high up on a pedal a stool
not caring if he has to revoke his hairitage.

In retrorespect
you could say that
        everybody looses

Arizona Suite

1

Sycamores in mottled bark
pose with oaks along the creek bed
below turrets of ochre north of Sedona.

Pine and juniper compose an air:
all is peach and sienna stone.

Burnt-orange cliff striations
sing verticality once and for all
into the geography of the heart.

One patch of gravity, cliff turret,
outrageously uplifted,
fills us like helium.

2

The Grand Canyon's whole breath-stopping gap.
Who was the first to see it?

Even with tourism and video cameras,
silence peels off layer after layer

where God keeps folding one hand
over the other, laying down paints.

A mauve moth flutters at the edge,
a crazy lizard skitters on the brink.

Our quarrels and misunderstandings.
This engulfs them.

3

Heading down into Verde Valley,
a sad helplessness is fine.

North of Phoenix, saguaro cactus
blooms like a candelabra.

Who cares if one is unhappy?
That little anguish too will pass.

4

I have felt safe in work,
but here work is tumbling

down a rockslide with the brown,
laughing children of Oak Creek.

Mapping the Human Genomes

Engineers map genomes of two bodies laid side by side:
the body physical, the body soul,

intermingling, nameless heaps.

When one lifts
     so the other

       when one descends

          there's a dropping.

Yet all that fingering cannot
discern the bright field

     (unknowable, illimitable)

        where they flare.

Celeste

You will never be a file clerk.

Your oasis mind
is too full of burning summer
tangerines

and your flying mantle
too exuberantly flung to the ground.

Your arms spill arabesques
from an abandoned temple
sprouting hyacinth and wisteria.

You are an Etruscan storm
breaking over white sand
where brown feet curl

and your body's pages
will not be locked
in metal drawers.

Heresies

Here is the heresy of the mind
rising above the body as if
the two had never been lovers.

As if there were no telltale musk,
no confluence of rivers, no
intertwining of hairs long and short.

Here is the heresy of the body
abandoning memory, excommunicate,
silenced down the stairstep spine.

But here too, somehow, the healing
communion of saints, the skin
a clear mirage, the body almost drinkable.

Here is the resurrection of the dead
in reservoirs of hearing,
aspens quaking in a wind's sarabande.

Here is the life everlasting –
generations gathered together
like sweet plums in a bowl.

The Listener

I am not a novelist, but if I were
I would not create characters,
rather, they would visit full-blown,
whispering in my ear their secrets
which I would cherish like blue light
spilled through tidal glass.

The musculature along my shoulders
would ache, then shiver into currents,
and my body, faithful Recording Angel,
would slide like a swimmer into their sea,
listening, uncensorious as water,
as they showed me their small wrists,

the grace of their swan-like hands.

Sisyphus, Kenotic

What if, in the midst of those nailed moments,
Sisyphus suddenly allowed himself to roll
down the hill with the stone,

in a sort of clownish somersaulting,
and pinwheeled like a child across earth-slope,
kenotic, and sprawled onto the trusted green?

What if, in the midst of these thrusts
of disparate, quirky time, the word
"perfect" suddenly became "ripe?"

If "ripe" became what you are most, here
in this Green, unfulfilled fulfilling?

Psyche

Obscure and rare that state to which I fell
or rose, no, floated awake into your invisible arms.

You whispered, *Désirée*, and touched me with a thousand
exquisite fingers – a rush like hummingbird wings

filtering through every parcel from crown to toe to crown,
crescendoing, falling, continuing night's extravagant enterprise

when we flowed and spiralled in the chakras of the spine,
blossomed in the thousand-petaled lotus of the brain.

You were not in and out and away like any ordinary lover,
but lingered all night, sequestering, calling me *Beloved*.

The Vision of God That Thou Dost See
Is My Vision's Greatest Enemy
– William Blake

What is it Yeats asked?
Are you content?
But who is ever content?

So her white hands beat
on that thick cloud.
Sharp darts of yearning

pierce up and up
over cedar roofs and cul-de-sacs
where there is yet

graciousness.
What then my soul?
Strap on your scarlet running shoes.

You are not flattened but
will fall like an exhausted dancer
some dim night

into that milky cloud.

A Dream of Thomas Merton

How is it the monk (unhabited) is not surprised,
sitting cross-legged on a patch of earth
trading jokes and cold beer?

Talk of Martin Luther King, Osama, fallen towers,
nothing new under the sun

(except his arch eyes, a high-energy discharge).

"Jesus was the kind of doctor
who would heal anyone who asked –
criminal, insane. No flinching or thinking of bounds."

He pronounces his own new name,
"Threshold Dweller" –
one who hops like Raven across portals.

Waking, I think how straightaway
I felt his mettle, knowing
he had been fed fire –

                    I, grain

Preceptor

(Spoken posthumously by Thomas Wentworth Higginson, who corresponded with Emily Dickinson)

Bulletins tumbled from evanescence.
She knew and did not know who she was.

You have not remembered me, as is fitting,
except as her dazed interlocutor,

her scanty peephole on the world.
My presumptuous critiquing of her poems

became my purgatory, now purged.
Even her epistles were nothing

but metaphor, cochineal under drab.
This quickened nobody wouldn't sign

but in pale strokes of pencil on a card,
as if to efface her name. Thankfully,

she did not absorb one whit of my advice:
"Get rid of the dashes – regularize the grammar."

Intensity played hide-and-seek with time,
genius volcanic in the interstices.

I was blind. I let her sign, "Your scholar,"
then, to my abiding glory, "Friend."

Had I died in the uncivil trenches of the South,
"Higginson" would be moribund.

Yet I survive in her wild – a man
who held, briefly galactic in his palm,

revolving *resonance of emerald,*
hummingbird in muslin's white.

Omega Suite

The greatest taboo is spirituality.
        – Carl Jung

1.
Light like cracked glass and the Christ
with his bucket of stars falling in our ears.

2.
The best thing he said, *The kingdom of heaven
is within you.*

3.
It is not God's anger undressing before you,
but your own enmity against the earth.

4.
I carry a small, white stone in my pocket,
and every time I rub it there's a prayer for you.

5.
Whatever they force on you won't be the thing –
whatever you find for yourself will be.

6.
The poet enters the particulars,
already a plenum,
antennae up, attending the flow.

A Liturgy of Creatures

You ask
who will
then take us
to the kingdom
which is
in heaven?
The birds
in the air,
the animals
on earth,
the fishes
in the streams
and the oceans.
They all shall
take you to
the heavenly kingdom
which is
in your heart.

– Egypt, 16th c. BCE

Psalm of the Open Secret

Holy One
> let your words sound in the crevasses of my speech.

Patient One
> sing your transformations
> even to the outermost cul-de-sacs of suburbia.

> When the leaves shoot out their tender paeans,
> wing my improbable transforming.

> Though my root remains silent,
> release my bloom into the attentive air.

> Because you have praised the world into being,
> I will praise you in the saturnine limbs of age.

> Compassion and Justice will kiss each other
> and all our works and days will be loved.

Holy One
> flexed in the arch of heron's neck,
> submerged in the squeals of the farmed mink,

> unnoticed in the fly swept from the ledge,
> teach me your animal names,

> bliss me your presence in the winged ones.

Monarch

A monarch butterfly
        unlaced from the languor of such long preparing,
                wings' sticky gauze,

amphibious (earth and sky),
        rapt to a midpoint, sweetened by
                gold laminate, black framed,

poised, not yet danced
        in cartwheels of light –
                that all and nothing thing.

Arachnids

levitate through their brief burgeoning,
        silkily cast,

armoured, lofted
        Knights Templar, ladies bountiful,

acrobats slung in silent safety nets,
        dancing highwires of verse

        skittering on a tensile of their own making.

Sea Turtle

floats up from circles of yellow trumpetfish
just in time to ignore
our small news of war and wounds.

(Indonesian tsunami sweeps away hundreds of thousands.)

White-Knight eyes
patrol paradise
(a slow suspension of oars,
      waltz of the woebegone),

coming only rarely up
      (graduate, summa cum laude)
            to loll in the common air.

Hare

Easy prey
frozen
reduced to naught but
the eerie canal of the ear.

      Squat brown hare
you, a sensitive
      to all playing in ectoplasm,
acclimatized to your element –
      constant angst,
quivering stasis,
except
      on this solstice momently,

        grandiloquent silence
rapt in sun stain.

Stellar's Jays

signal no more
than a flicker of blue

flung sapphires.

          Still – they pierce.

Chickadee

Black-capped chickadee
       (fleshed messenger and message)
startles an inner dullness.

Trill summons my meditation,
lifts it
over the steering wheel and beyond the car.

Small feet braced
eyes flecked
with quick intent.

Dear bird,
return and draw again
       that keening song,
       that circling kaddish on loan to air.

Crow

I am pith of pine,
aromatic laughter,

arboreal anthem
spiralling beyond hearing,

never-to-be-quenched fire
in the heart of home,

full fling of wing
everywhere dark in light, light in dark –

a rambunctious tremor.

In a Heron's Silence

Heron's silence
       against invisible ruckus of crows.

Mink farm stench –
       Langley's death camp.

Doomed Angus gather –
       hillside Quixotes.

Wing-flapping ostriches –
       crazy conductors.

Squirrel's prehensile tail
       curls in my spine.

Dog

Crouched at our camps,
sleeping in our caves,

tethered, corded, leashed
companion in the hunt.

If we bow and bow,
we cannot atone

for the dodge, the cringe.
Your romp and drool,

fully moment-wise,
teach us to relish loam –

you, Nose of Creation,
rolling tumult in grass,

vocabulary unencompassed
by "come," "sit," and "stay."

Kindred Kine

Two lopsided cows
knuckle-kneed
flick droning flies
and lick each other's
wind-weathered sides,
capsizing at dusk
under the hill.

Two heads lift
as a woman passes.

Grooming resumes,
joint leanings
one into the other,
a shelter of tongues.

Who is to say these companions
inclining toward dark
do not move those soft tongues
against the day of their slaughter?

Ram on Moriah

I am a library of bleats,
Torah of pain,
ram almost slain,
Abraham's scapegrace fool,

not canny enough to evade
the servant's hands
or eye of tyrant and his cold god.

May the voice in his head
that arrested his dagger
and freed the boy
speak again:

Lay not thy hand upon the ram.
The Holy One requires only
justice and a pure heart.

Moth

On a white ledge
       arrayed in a beige silk shift

your wings
       (strophe and antistrophe)
              inside the morning light.

How you evaded webs, lightbulbs, brooms,
       laid yourself out
           in stippled breaths,

surrendered
       to this flowing light
           travelling from the one to the one,

so now
       all that matters is
           the colour of the soul.

End of a Most Beautiful Poem Heard in Sleep

Who from here can surmise
the pure wide sweeps of sand,
the animals' night rotations?

The Works and Days of the Non-Human

Spaniel, my spiritual director,
praise be to you, yoked
to the two-leggeds in work and play,

and to you Rufous-sided Towhee,
apogee of instinct, whose plunge
into green light annihilates time.

Praise to ant, persistent thief
of crumbs and litter,
bead-eyed bravery.

Glory to you orb weaver,
mending with your small hands
time's spindrift threads.

Glory to hummingbird,
vermillion-throated Ezekiel,
Merkabah mystic, wheel within Wheels.

Glory to songbird,
voicefall, master librettist
(yours the pure, ours the demotic tongue).

And to wolf in mindful meditation,
wild arrogance, aplomb
going it alone against a field's shadow.

And to you cow, scholar of death,
Hamlet-like ruminator
deep in your vow of stability.

And geese in a cloud of unknowing
with naked intent beating against night,
dream-lofted sailors.

Yours the works and days
(small in great; great in small)
squall and joy tumbling together.

Lifting the Stone

Advent

Resist the pace imposed.
Culture (as with malign intent)

fears the boundless,
something that if unleashed

might overthrow dominions
and set up in the Mercy Seat

that frowning, burning babe.

Recalling the Words

Call back "reform" as sky's releasing wisps
of cumulus that stir around a peak
in constant re-formation of the world.

Re-call "spirit," a deep and constant breath
within the cell, both summons and command
to fire the body from its diamond caves.

And last, restore the subtle mystery
in "god," imploring one, light in a dog,
or cedar drapery, shining thread, deus,

in father, mother, woman, beast and stone,
sustaining presence rapt within the gold.

The Tasks

Who coordinates this awesome spectacle
of concept, object, thought and weighty task?

How long can such a marshalling cohere
as it does, suspended in midair?

No, I am not coherent or even half alive,
but dreaming perplexed stones uphill in stony sleep.

Lifting the Stone

Lift up the stone, and you will find me there.
            – The Gospel of Thomas

Suddenly from the very pivot
of wrenching horror – forgiveness,

a shift, a loosening.
One death enters the only world.

Suddenly
past talk of atonement and sin

one dies in this very death
I carry in my arms.

Suddenly it is clear
what must be done
            and why the voice says,

        Do nothing.

Not quietism this,
for in the dust
        motes dance.

            She has been under the rocks
            and in the hard places of dreams

        to record the most peripheral arabesques.

Besotted with Jesus

Still besotted with Jesus after all these years
despite the unfashionableness of such love
unconscionable history of the Church
sad path of pillage, persecution, crusade
racism, war and rumours of war.

Despite heart horrors held in continuance
      some record and reverberation extends
          shimmering to the enemy (ourselves).

What a Mediterranean peasant began
remains untried
except in the shock and awe of saints

those human frailties, marginal men and women
      (Francis, Teresa, Gandhi, Mandela, Weil)

stunning the warrior Hate
          (healers, transformers).

Call me Christian Jew Buddhist Hindu Sufi
      (whatever you like)

big fruit salad of the Spirit
      every flavour savoured

          drenched in a common juice
          culled in unnamable mind

          (Krishna Waka Tanka Gaia Dionysius Sophia)
          Peerless Peer

all and none of the above.

Cross Piece

Event now fading as if cross-hatched,
    strands of hair across ashen face,
        whipping wind and pissing stench –

the worst humans can do – similar in all climates.
    But how am "I" impressed on the straightened scene,
        a roving camera's eye?

This figure of my attention stuns and stuns.
    "I" a small fly on the crosspiece
        braced for pith and pain.

Words fly: *forgive them.* Breath sweetens
    the dark imagination. (We have been told
        the war is not in these suburbs where comfort lies.)

Why then do I stumble in midnight's dream
    over a dismembered female breast?
        Why this envelope of shame, this stain on plenty's brow?

Clotted fire in the blood, perpetual now.
    No wholesome prayer, no private voice, no safeguard safe
        until we say as one – *war no more.*

Portals swing, something shifts in the atmosphere,
    rends inner space,
        cracks ceiling and floor.

Two songbirds in a tree – one singing, one listening:
    I am with you in the utmost beginning.
        A skimming of sound, whorls in the thumb.

Sparrows in the crosspiece and naked children, one on every branch
    where love goes with them down piecemeal,
        pierced, peaced, sprawled and splintered here.

Why Christos of the Caverns?

Because someone mastered heartlore,
      whispered in my inner ear, Beloved,
            bathed me all night in a spa of kisses

and is lovely, a paroxysm of grace,
      claimed me so I had no choice but to love;
            because of an overwhelming devotion even
                to the sound of the name,

because wherever that one is, there am I,
      because he does not confine himself to the lists,
            because I am a solitary cell in that bright body,

because I fall to phoenix ash.

Mary Mother

She must have seen the blunt nose of death
when he set his face steadily toward Jerusalem,
and perhaps it was right and perhaps
there was no other way.

Yet the sword,
so long impaled in her heart,
slipped, turned its edge
against the inner chamber,
and the body that had so irrevocably said yes
to such a long-executed consumption
writhed in frozen light,
friable carving
sculpted of sheer pain.

Secret Drift

Dear journal, to whom I confide my all,
dear messy, chaotic orderings,
dear shelf life, lifeline, capacious soul,
roll call of grief, catalogue of abjection,
derelict scribe, blank slate
humbler than thou, lined with leaves,
coffee-stained, dog-eared gropings in dark,

now I will confide something worth your knowing.

Unable to accept the God-face of a tyrant of my making
who must be appeased by blood of ram or human,
I missed the import of Jesus' brutal death.

A callous wind – a hurricane whooshes in.

One disconsolate downward look
absorbs the fallow eyes, unhallowed ignorance
and breathes   *forgive.*

Something flips,
fear repents,
love's gravitation
            catches a dead galaxy in its spiral.

Query

What if St. Francis had sought the birds and said,
     "Preach to me,"
or to the Saracens,
     "I surrender the God I call mine?"

Shame

1

Each day the music
whether we will or no.

Outside, magnolia's unfurling
slims the air

even now uniting the worlds we are,
one divided current,

heads devouring hearts, heads
marching backwards as to war:

"Hallelujah, glory, gory, hallelujah."
"Holy holy holy," saith the wind.

Shame falls out of the sky.
Crash helmets, gas masks, tanks,

hungry voices of children in the loaded air.
Who will heal the frightened enemy – "ourself?"

Stockmarket graphs – barometers of greed.
"Shock and awe" of terror's inhuman blast

unveils no weapons of mass destruction
but our own.

2

Across from the Langley Colossus,
tranced faces munch burgers
while Baghdad blazes
on screens one and two,
the hockey game on screen three.

Thank God it's finally Friday
and off to the movies for something
vicariously violent or
maybe a "chick flick"
to distract from the horror that is
our daily bread.

3

Here on the lawn, Magnolia, lover, beloved,
shudders to her roots

knowing April will swell in her again,
releasing love's ample white blossoms

once more into the unreceiving atmosphere.

Midwifery

When my mother tripped the light fantastic,
I stood as midwife,

culled words that released her
as she hovered a while above my head,

listening as I bespoke
the silent bedframe.

She dressed herself then in syllables,
redressed in a bed of vowels,

watched my brother circle
the room's narrowing square.

All was clear now,
for nothing could separate the love-filled.

A pair of freckled arms
led her out to the Christ,

an amber man on a soft divan
who whispered,

The place of your deepest resistance
is the place of your deepest healing.

Postures of Surrender

Sitting
arms aloft
kneeling
prostrate
palm to palm as holy palmers
palms open
palms crossed
hands a tower, a church
the temple (body) silent
ready to lower its obdurate head

> postures of surrender
> postures of unknowing
> postures of unposturing

> kissing the ground

Luminous Companion

how we project on your inimitable face
the faces of our wishes, irritations, fears.

O Luminous Companion,

how you shuttle us station after station
from subliminal dark to supernal shock,

casting off the veils we throw over your features,
weaving the shroud you tear, and tear again.

One day, you mend these lendings,
the next, consign them to flame,

exposing a new wardrobe of shimmering sheaths.

O Luminous Companion,

how silently you take your place with us at supper,
how sweetly you moisten our parched lips

and place *visionlieder* in our chests,
till we are singing not from the throat only

but chanting from the follicles of all hairs.

O Luminous Companion,
                              stay.

I had not known
each step would bring both pain and bliss

and you – containing all –
                              who wash a wider-windowed sky.

Getting Naked with God

is where it all leads
whatever it is
and he is not of course a he
and the pillow talk is dark
but not unseemly
because when you get naked with God
you put all your confessions on hold
and get down and of course
naked as a newly-fired babe
empty as an evacuated oyster shell
exposing your heart to this one
who blows your cares to dust
with your plans
lovingly of course
and is tired of talking
and wants to get down, down
which is in, further and deeper in
but you keep saying
here/there, you/me
though desire pants like a hart
and a song preoccupies your mindscape
a longing song long forgotten
and remembered and forgotten again
and you are very young
and unstudied and callow
for you have dropped everything
for this oneness
which is not in time
for this, which
is not named
for this which is
this   this
burning channelling

Radiant Body

For as the soul is a being of the cosmic order, it is
absolutely necessary that it should have an estate
or portion of the cosmos in which to keep house.
    – Philoponus

Perhaps heaven shelters in this elbow
resting on this desk, where hand cradles chin,
      or out there in Orion thoughts intend
      to lean into this place and grow
lungs, or go four-footed, or on wings,
so says the circulating word that sings

news from nowhere, mystery in the wheels,
surprise – whatever awakened Ezekiel
      who though broken, half in hell
      considered no negotiations, no deals.
If all of me belongs in several worlds,
when body ages and leaf-like curls

it is possible some radiant skin
will flare within this flesh,
      a denser light, forgotten guest
      arise familiar like lost kin.
What if earth houses more than we know –
some subtle-bodied dream of long ago?

What I Will Not Remember

from the cylinder of my days
is tossing earlier drafts of poems
into the blue recycling bag on Thursday night,
wondering what will flip before me
at breath's precipice, and where
the unwanted lines will go,
imagining some desperate soul picking
through garbage bags, finding
and reading them, amused, enchanted
or only disappointed they aren't coupons.

I will not remember the day
I rifled through my daughter's desk
owning the problem of her homework,
or the stir fry at the college cafeteria
with too much peanut-satay sauce
that set me choking over conversation
about a colleague in palliative care.

I will not remember the sun anointing my face
the day I lay stretched on the floral comforter,
snuggling back in for more sleep,
prickly light in my spine,
thinking myself lucky to be alive,
my family in the next room.

Who will enter the trivial, forgotten moments,
wondering how poetry reconstructs memory
and walks with it, oriflamme, through time's gaps?

Faith Is the Evidence

faith is the evidence of things
faith is the evidence of things not
faith is the evidence of naught
faith is the evidential naughting
faith is things
a robin-blue egg
a spotted frog's leaping
faith is the leap
right over the round world
into the not
faith, faith is
the rounded opening
faith is the text
intuited before the read word
faith is the bird in the heart not the hand
the thing with feathers
shaking and empty
thought of a thought
stretched, faithful
to the round, unhatched
that struggles without aim
to caress night, the dark
eye converted from sight
to lack, the unattached, invisible
faith evidenced here
in one renourished cell
plumped, resolute
vocation of cells to be
and not be in the field
the moving field that utters
yes maybe no
faith things the world
peoples the other with palest wings
advocates for a widening
dares the abyss
faiths
where substance leans into things
reclines, a faithful friend

O invisible one
          your sheen

In a Room Called Resurrection

A young and a middle-aged woman
are cupped in sleep.

In a room called waking
walls open to corridors,

give way to antechambers
and quiet terrariums,

solariums where tent caterpillars
meander up and down

through tender shoots, choosing
the most ordinary leaves,

softly denting the foliage
with small persistent mouths.

Monarch butterflies weave
slow paths in air, and above

drops of sun swirl
and walls collapse,

slung octaves of flowerbeds
like hidden stairs spiralling.

Seven Ways of Looking at the Kingdom Prayer

1

Ubiquitous Presence,

let your realm descend
(ours being so small).

Your will be done
(ours, too limited).

Help us locate our will
within yours

till earth is perceived
as it is, heaven,

where all things are unified
beyond our separatist notions.

Let us dance in the grand hullabaloo,
not muting the music.

Give us this day what we most need,
knowing everything flows from you,

and walk with us steadily to
the great self-emptying.

Be close when mortmain calls,
you, our deepest interiority,

dancing still on the green.

2

Burning One,
you, flaming in earth and in heaven,

holy in luminosity,
holy in darkness.

Let your presence so blaze
that there is no more difference

between your kingdom
and the kingdoms of this world.

Let us feed the hungry
till no one is malnourished,

and help us circulate
more constantly in the deep forgiving.

Keep us from self-alienation
which hides our original faces from us.

Ache in us for justice
till you set up a tent in our hearts

forever.

3

Dearest Helper,
Author, Muse, Matrix,

we are your far-flung flotsam,
fortuitous night-seed,

stanza without end –
time's branching poem.

Amen, amen.

4

For parents who wounded unknowingly –
a child's forgiveness.

For those not yet healed of childhood trauma –
self-love.

For the closed fist –
grace.

For those desiring a sterile outward order rather than
the fecund tumble of chaos –
fearlessness.

For the riot of names that is God's unnameable body –
vision.

For a sweep of sand carved by an aqua sea –
awe.

5

O Holy One,
expand our cramped encampments.

Lower your world so imperceptibly into ours,
the two become one in our perceiving.

Help us to take only what we need
and embrace us in the endless conjoining.

Open our hearts in the turmoil
and keep us permeable to your spirit.

6

Welcome, Holy Presence,
You who unite heaven and earth.

Feed us, your fledglings, release us
into the cornucopia air

where there is no "mine" and "yours."
Break upon us

when we slip on the stair.

Propel our propositions
like scrolls into the sea.

Rescue us from opinion.
Transmute our desire

and make us again, beginners.

7

Our Mother,

holy in matter,
matter in us again.

You, sea spray and firework,
calm keeper of geological ages.

Dignify our cells.
Place us once more among the order of wild things.

Water Corona

Water Corona

1

To meditate on water in her many transformations –
runnel's zest, creek's crouch, waterfall's
leap, glacier's gathered tears,
the promises of wells –
is a privilege of the hydrated,
but those whose cells pant
for water's deepest ministry
cry for a dram to parched throats,
flow that embraces the human
and more than human worlds.
So, it is our luck to contemplate
the pure springs of dreams,
to wake, thirsting, fill a glass brim-full,
enjoy what is not limitless balm.

2

What is not limitless balm arose
from a limitless source, dense heart
bursting from the original fireball.
How is it a galaxy of fiery arms
nourished such bonding? Who married
your molecules in a streaming bed
and sang their epithalamion to the stars?
Gaia, dressed in dripping firmaments,
announced your arrival, wrapped you
in a receiving blanket of blue silk.
Islands floated on your primordial
stream, whose depths bred starfish,
butterfly fish, crab, coral, sea anemone,
a turbulence from which we might not have emerged.

3

A turbulence from which we might not have emerged
became your journeywork; cells said your name
and we swam forth, abandoning our fishy tails.
Your pulse in the amniotic caves
was a canyon-carving softness.
Soon sky reflected your greys and greens.
When you enacted your birth in our bodies,
you graced us with mineral springs,
underground streams, secret grottos
for our ablutions and ceremonies,
lifting us up and dipping us down
in the rivers of your voice.
Mother, matrix – licking the newborn
with your large wet tongue.

4

With your large wet tongue,
you gentle us, tend us as we drop
from your side, cooling our foreheads.
Soon we climb, bearing our sweat and gear
up the peak to find you stretched
solitary between mountains, startling
our possibilities with glacial blue.
Despoilers of such wild reserve –
contenders, dumpers, extractors
from a mechanistic school – build dams
over and against your living body,
pronounce you "other," marked for our use.
Eagle, with knife-edge skill, plummets deep,
feeds in your empire, while we drown in our own.

5

Feeding in your empire, while we drown in our own,
the animals enter the slow crucifixions of water.
Children retreat from shore, deer shrink
from creeks. Fertilizers, pesticides,
car emissions infect your pores,
the water cycle breaks on its wheel,
condensation falls as acid rain
on the keening heads of whales.
Valleys flood and dry at human command.
Underground springs, your last refugees,
fugitive, crouching in your dark,
sense computers plotting
the extraction of your marrow –
though one living drop could save the world.

6

Though one living drop could save the world,
we stop our ears to your music.
Water ascends angelic
in the stems of roses, descends
over cliffs in self-abandonment.
Nothing is more humble than water,
brother, sister, seeking the lowest place,
washer of feet, and of our souls,
those reservoirs, containing us,
shaping our bodies' fluid estate.
Though we boil in cauldrons,
hibernate in cisterns, sink stiff-necked in ice,
your forms continue melting
snow's white compact around the heart.

7

Snow's white compact around the heart
numbs, and private greed for public
gift may extinguish our species.
"Let justice flow like water," says the prophet.
When polar icecaps melt, climates climax,
and floods ransack the world,
who will choose – now – this day –
to bend to water's ways?
Becoming tributaries to water, we
might serve what eye cannot fathom,
mysterious in her mingling with earth,
air, fire – Thales' Elemental Queen,
hydrosphere hymned in this meditation
on water in her myriad transformations.

Notes

27   **Sisyphus**, in Greek mythology, was a cruel king of Corinth condemned for eternity to roll a boulder up a hill only to have it roll down again just before it reached the top.

27   **Kenosis** is a term used in the New Testament, usually translated "emptying;" a form of generous self-donation that imitates the compassionate self-giving of the cosmos.

44   **Merkabah** is used in *Ezekiel* (1:4-26) to refer to the throne-chariot of God, the four-wheeled vehicle driven by four creatures, each with four wings and four faces (of a man, lion, ox, and eagle).

63   **Philoponus** was a 6th century Alexandrian grammarian and theologian; commentator on Aristotle.

81   **Thales** was a Greek pre-Socratic philosopher whose most famous belief was his cosmological doctrine, which held that the world originated from water.

Acknowledgements

Gratitude to Catherine Owen, Katerina Fretwell, Russell Thornton, David Zieroth, and John Porter for the inestimable gift of their thoughtful responses to this manuscript in its various stages. Thanks to Allan Briesmaster at Seraphim for his meticulous editing and to Maureen Whyte for her kind support.

"If I/I Will" in *Transition* (an annual publication of the Canadian Mental Health Association).

"Brother" in *Contemporary Verse 2*.

"Summer Godlore" and "Omega Suite" in *The New Orphic Review*.

"Three Vegetarians Visit a Venison Farm" in *Coastlines III* (White Rock and Surrey Writers' anthology).

"Cribbed from My Students' Essays" in *The Windsor Review*.

"Arizona Suite" and "Mapping the Human Genomes" in *Hammered Out* (Hamilton Poetry Society).

"Celeste" in *Hook and Ladder*.

"Heresies" in *The Harpweaver*.

"Organon" (previously titled "I Note") in *The Cormorant*.

"The Listener" in *Quarter Moon Quarterly*.

"Psyche" in *White Wall Review*.

"The Vision of God That Thou Dost See" in *Pottersfield Portfolio*.

"Preceptor" and "Shedding and Clinging" in *The Antigonish Review*.

"Psalm of the Open Secret" in the anthology *Writing the Sacred: A Psalm-Inspired Path to Appreciation and Writing Sacred Poetry*. Ed. Ray McGinnis (Northstone Publishing, 2005).

"The Tasks," "Advent" and "What I Will Not Remember" in *Canadian Literature*.

"Besotted with Jesus" and "Mary Mother" in *The Journal of Feminist Studies in Religion*.

"Water Corona" in *Voices Across Boundaries: a Multifaith Review of Current Affairs*.

"Luminous Companion" in *Palabras Press* (online).

"Preceptor" is to be published in the *Sandburg-Livesay Anthology* through Unfinished Monument Press.

"A Liturgy of Creatures" in *Poetry and Liturgy* (St. Thomas Poetry Society, 2007).

"Faith Is the Evidence" was the first place winner in the Burnaby Writers' Society Annual Poetry Contest for 2005.

"A Dream of Thomas Merton" was the grand prize winner of the *Presence* annual poetry contest, 2006 and was published in *Presence: An International Journal of Spiritual Direction.*

"Radiant Body" was the first-place winner of the Federation of BC Writers' 18th Annual Literary Writes Competition for 2006. "Faith Is the Evidence" was a finalist in the same contest and published in *Wordworks* (Federation of B.C. Writers, Winter 2006).

"In a Room Called Resurrection" won honourable mention in the 2006 Silver Hammer Poetry Contest of *Hammered Out.*

The ancient Egyptian poem used as the epigraph to "A Liturgy of Creatures" came to me via Dundas, Ontario sculptor Wayne Allan.

Other Books by Susan McCaslin

Locutions. Victoria, B.C.: Ekstasis Editions, 1995.

Light Housekeeping. Victoria, B.C.: Ekstasis Editions, 1997.

Veil/Unveil. Toronto: The Saint Thomas Poetry Series, 1997.

Into the Open. Port Moody, B.C.: Golden Eagle Press, 1999.

Flying Wounded. Gainesville, Florida: The University Press of Florida, 2000.

The Altering Eye. Ottawa, Ontario: Borealis Press, 2000.

Common Longing: The Teresa Poems and A Canticle for Mary and Martha. New York: Mellen Poetry Press, 2001.

At the Mercy Seat. Vancouver, B.C.: Ronsdale Press, 2003.

A Plot of Light. Lantzville, B.C.: Oolichan Press, 2004.